LEAVE YOUR IMPRIN

STEPOUT

JONATHAN A. MERRITT

FOREWORD BY BISHOP ANDREW MERRITT

TABLE OF CONTENTS

DEDICATION

To my loving wife, Tatianna
and my three adorable children,
Lillian, Cristina, and Andrew II.
It's all for you.

FOREWORD

What you're holding in your hands today is not a motivational speech, laced with pompoms and whistles. Each word, and every line, is a promise—my promise—bruised, yet birthed.

I distinctly remember the fresh snow that had fallen the night before. A crisp December moment etched in my mind forever.

"Mr. Merritt?"

"Yes."

"Do you have a son in the Caribbean, sir?"

"Yes."

"Is your son's name, Jonathan?"

"Yes, it is."

"Sir, I'm sorry to call you like this…your son Jonathan has died."

For a split second, I felt something I have never felt before. I am not sure how to describe it. What I do remember was how every instrument in my car became cloudy in an instant. The tears had filled my eyes before I could comprehend what was happening in that moment.

Step Out!

Was this what Jacob in the Bible felt, when his sons stood before him, telling him that his son, Joseph, was gone? He hadn't gotten a chance to tell him goodbye. He wasn't there to whisper, "I love you, son." Was my son alone, or was there someone with him while my promise was being extracted from this earth?

In a flash, I saw Abraham climbing that mountain with wood, a weapon, and his promise in tow.

My mind was racing. Through tears and praying in the Spirit, I immediately grabbed the phone and called my son's phone number.

No answer. (I took a deep breath.)

I dialed again.

No answer.

Random thoughts raced through my mind.

My son is the product of a promise that God made to me. "In you the nations of the earth will be blessed. Your ministry will reach your city, your nation, and world for Jesus Christ." I knew that the promise of reaching the world for Jesus Christ was to extend beyond my lifetime.

I had four lovely daughters by the time his mother conceived. This time was different. I was believing for a son to carry on the Merritt name.

Foreword

(Still calling.)

No answer.

I was thinking how God had answered every prayer and fulfilled every word concerning my boy to this point. I had stood on the Word and boldly declared to everyone who would listen that there was a boy in my wife's womb and that he would be born on my birthday! (Smiling as the tears ran down my face.)

See you don't understand that back in 1982 there was no ultrasound to tell you the sex of the baby. There was only faith to step out on.

(Calling his brother now. Phone ringing...no answer.)

My mind went back to the day he was born. Yes, the doctor had given us a due date of December 4th. But we knew he was wrong, because **my** son was going to born on **my** birthday, November 28th. And it was so.

Prepping my wife's bag, the Saturday night before my birthday, I asked, "Honey, do you know what tomorrow is?"

"Yes. It's the day I'm having our son." That's right!

A few hours later at 7:22 am on Sunday morning, my baby boy entered the earth. My promise fulfilled. (I knew exactly how Abraham felt the moment he saw Isaac.)

Step Out!

My son has become the subject of many of my messages over the years including, *You Can Have What You Say* and *Faith Extenders*. He is the promise of God fulfilled to me.

So, I kept calling his phone.

You must be thinking, "Why call a child that you were told was dead?"

Because promises don't die.

My faith had brought me to this moment, and it held on to what God had spoken over my son regardless of what anyone else said. The Spirit of God in me knew what I couldn't articulate.

But I was going to hear my baby boy's voice again— somehow.

Suddenly, the phone rang!

It was his brother...

"David, have you heard from your brother?"

"Well, um, no, Dad," my son David said.

"Call your brother and tell him to call me."

"Oh, ok. I will."

After getting off the phone with David, I thought back through a life of moments with my son. Then my heart turned to all the parents who had buried their children during decades of ministry. I officiated. I encouraged. And I had prayed with hundreds of parents, never really knowing the depth of their loss.

But in that millisecond, I knew exactly what they felt. An unbelievable shriek of disbelief. And though I understood the impact of the loss, I couldn't allow myself to stay there.

Ring. Ring. Ring.

"Dad? Hi, Dad. David said you wanted me to call you."

I don't even remember picking up the phone.

"Son!"

The tears of joy and thankfulness had all weaved together at that moment. I couldn't speak, and yet I could.

Without hesitation, I said, "I love you son. I just want you to know that I love you."

Overwhelmed by the magnitude of it all. I couldn't describe the details of what had just happened. I didn't share it with my wife, my church, or my other children until a more appropriate time.

"I'll talk to you when you get back son. I love you."

"I love you too, Dad."

After hanging up the phone, I started to reflect.

Step Out!

Stepping out on a promise means you must get out of the way and trust the Word that has been spoken to you. Knowing that the integrity of His word is strong enough to hold you up through anything that comes to challenge it.

When I hung up the phone that day, I had to make a decision whether to succumb to what I heard or move in what I knew about the Word concerning my seed.

Instead, I focused on the promise from God to me, and the promise of God over his life. In doing so, my wife and I collectively and individually acknowledge that the central theme of our lives is Jesus. His purpose. His plan. His promise.

Because little did we know that a month later another call was coming. We had to pray and believe God again for our child, just like any other parent would do. But I knew whatever had happened, "It was not unto death." Because promises from God don't die.

However, like many people who have a promise from God, pain is part of the package. There will be trials and tribulations that come to challenge every promise of God to you. The trials and tribulations come to perfect your faith, not halt your movement.

With this understanding, stepping out from where you are into the flow of where He is becomes a journey of sweet satisfaction, peace, and unspeakable joy. Knowing this: there is no surer foundation than stepping out in faith as you walk out the Word that has been spoken to you.

Allow this book to be a coach of encouragement and a written testament of the faithfulness of God. Find yourself in these pages, but more importantly, my prayer is that you find the heart of God's love in them.

Refuse to let this be just another book you place on your shelf, vowing to read another day. Take this testimony, this journey, this faith, and apply it to where you are in your life right now. Or, share it with someone that you know would benefit from the significance of these events.

My son is not allowing his wounds to be wasted. He is sharing his scars with you as a tool to help someone else. As a father and pastor, I am grateful for the powerful love of the Father, who saw a crossroad of two hills and a death sentence but chose to exchange His son for mine.

It's with that confidence that I am unwavering as I encourage you to step out on whatever God has spoken to you. No matter how far it takes you or how many challenges come, He will not leave you to go through them alone.

So go ahead, stretch your muscles, and move forward into the perfected promises that God has for you.

Step Out!

Always remember, promises don't die—they persevere.

Step out.

Yours In the Yoke of the Master,

Bishop Andrew Merritt

PREFACE

As I look back, I had been burning the candle at both ends for a while. Between my ministry duties, both administrative and pastoral, my obligations to my thriving new business, and the need to be both available and engaged for my wife and children, I knew it was time to take a moment away, to relax and enjoy some 'downtime' with my wife.

All I can tell you is that one minute, I was having a wonderful time on the beautiful island of Costa Rica and the next I was being loaded in a vehicle nearly unconscious and completely unaware of the challenges that lay ahead of me in the coming weeks.

I had been blindsided.

There was no way of getting around the fact that I had been sucker punched out of nowhere. Have I had situations in my life that required me to move forward when all I wanted to do was shrink back, withdraw from everyone and everything—wounded and disappointed? Of course. But this, my friends, was different. This was an assault so horrific and unexpected that everyone standing in proximity to me not only heard the impact, but they felt it too.

My wife and I had just enjoyed a delicious meal on the beach. The moon was as bright as I had ever seen in my lifetime. There were so many stars and the smell of the salty breeze coming off the water was the perfect setting to what I saw as a glorious vacation up to this point.

After dinner, our driver arrived to take us back to the resort. I was more than excited to enjoy the beauty of Costa Rica with my love. At one point in our ride back, we began to proceed up a long hill, slowing climbing to the top.

As we reached the top of the hill, there was a sprinkler that began to hit the golf cart with water. The driver slowly started to reverse the vehicle that we were riding in. Suddenly he changed gears and we started moving forward. Unexpectedly, the wheels of the cart started to spin uncontrollably, which forced the front of the cart to begin to lift off the ground.

My wife and I were violently ejected from the back of the cart, tumbling down the hill.

For five minutes after initial impact, I couldn't comprehend what had just happened. What I did know was that "The angel of the Lord encamps [settles in, lodges, and pitches tents] all around those that fear him, and delivers them," (Psalm 34:7 NKJV). I couldn't see a thing because of how dark it was on that hill.

Preface

"God answer you on the day you crash, the name God-of-Jacob put you out of harm's reach, send reinforcements from [His] Holy Hill." (Psalms 20:1-2 MSG)

But God had already prepared for that day with a military force of angels securing a perimeter of protection around me. And the good news is that He has done the same for you.

The enemy is no match for the angelic force that God has assembled and assigned on your behalf. Yes, there are times when satan is foolish enough to throw a punch in your direction, but there is no blow that he tries to land that will ever supersede the plan of God for your life.

Satan thought that he had a strategy to eliminate Jesus. But guess what? His scheme backfired big time. His influence over the rulers of the age at that time had no understanding of the secret wisdom of God.

"Which none of the rulers of this age knew; for had they known, they would not have crucified the Lord of glory," (1 Corinthians 2:8). If satan had any clue what God was going to do with a crucified Jesus and a resurrected Jesus, there is no way he would have pushed for His execution. But that's the point: he didn't know.

God has intentions for my life that I cannot comprehend. That's why the enemy's attempted murder plot against me didn't work. Because just like he couldn't kill Jesus, he has no power to kill me. Nor does he have the power to kill you.

I know he had a tombstone ready to read:

1982-2018
Jonathan Andrew Merritt
Husband, Father, Son, Pastor
Beloved by the Straight Gate Church

He was ready to celebrate the grief that my family and friends would have experienced over my transition to glory. But God said, "Not so!" Because not only do I belong *to* Jesus, He lives *in* me! Jesus is still alive *in* me! If you are a believer, He is alive *in* you! Satan has no power to take your life, just like he didn't have the power to take His.

"No one takes it from me, but I lay it down of my own accord. I have authority to lay it down and authority to take it up again." (John 10:18)

Do you understand the power that we have on the inside of us? "The same Spirit that raised Jesus from the dead will quicken [make alive] your mortal body," (Romans 8:11). When I stood up on that dark road in Costa Rica—I wasn't standing on my own. The SAME Spirit that raised Jesus from the DEAD had quickened MY mortal body.

Imagine me lying there nearly unconscious. I did not have feeling in my right arm or right leg. They were both completely numb. My elbow was deformed—busted open and bleeding for over 24 hours after the accident. I was dazed, not able to comprehend where I was or what was happening to me at the time. It looked like I was down, and it was all over.

Maybe it looks the same for you. You are not the only one that satan is trying to take out. He makes attempts on all of us, whenever he finds an opportunity. Don't be discouraged. Because as sure as our God lives, you are going to make it. The angels have set-up and pitched tents around you, too. All because you belong to Jesus!

As I was lying on that Costa Rican hill limp and lifeless. An SUV was riding up the hill to finish me off. However, the angels had set a perimeter of protection around me, and the Spirit of God was quickening my mortal body!

I spent the remainder of my vacation in a hospital bed. Having multiple x-rays taken. Several IV's being administered, and pain killers being shot into various areas of my body, all in an effort to stop my nerves from shooting on all cylinders.

You've got to see the scene here. You must get this in your spirit because this is not a random blessing exclusively for me. No, no, no...this is what God is doing for all of us!

Step Out!

Your days are not finished upon this earth, and you will rise and declare God's glory. Your story is not over, and the next chapter has only just begun.

CHAPTER ONE: STUCK

Come, sit with me. Let's chat for a moment.

Lately, I've noticed that you've been going around in circles a bit. It's like you've been stuck in a holding pattern of sorts. You're acting as if your communication with the control tower is not working properly. I see your activity, but it's been lackluster as of late. I've wanted to say something before. However, I wanted to be careful not to offend you in the process.

Nonetheless, I was reminded that, "If we see [you] a man overtaken in a fault, you which are spiritual, restore such a one in the spirit of gentleness; considering yourself, lest you also be tempted." (Galatians 6:1 NKJV)

Now, before you get offended, the word *fault* according to *Webster's 1828 Dictionary* doesn't just mean *"sin or willful action."* It also means, *"whatever impairs excellence."* In Greek, it is translated as, *"to side slip, lapse or deviation; unintentional error."*

Know that I am not attacking your character here. This is about us, you and me, coming together to make a difference for God and to see His plans for our lives fulfilled. My goal is to help—that's all that's happening here.

I have asked God to use me to help others, so goes my heart to help.

Step Out!

As I write this the nerves in my body are on the fritz! They are firing on all cylinders. Yes, I have pain medications, prayer, holistic remedies, hot showers, cold baths, natural herbs and spices, all being employed to calm my body down.

Ironically, I major in calm. I know stress-free living, mind, body, and soul. After all, I own a company built around the simplicity of a stress-free lifestyle. Yet, my body is behaving like it didn't get the memo. Still, I refuse to get stuck.

But I don't want to talk about me right now. I want to talk about you.

In saying that, it seems like you're at the same altitude as you were last year and the year before that too. My goal in bringing this up is so that we can talk this out and maybe get to the root of the problem. I don't want you to be in this same place this time next year. I want to see buds of the gifts and goals of God in you coming forth.

Don't laugh. I'm serious. Just like you, I want to see some manifestations come forth in my life as well. So right now, let's commit to going forward together, by taking this pledge.

"I, _____, commit to going forward, so that I may witness manifestations of God in my life."

Chapter One: Stuck

On my part, I know that I had times when I was stuck. You know that feeling of going nowhere slow. Just the same routine day after day—existing; doing nothing exciting really.

For me, it first came from a disappointing shoulder injury in college. It took me a minute to regroup after I realized I would not have the professional basketball career I had been preparing for most of my life.[1]

Since I was three years old, watching basketball with my father, I had been obsessed with the game. I remember watching Michael Jordan play, mesmerized by his skills. His ability to handle the ball. The way he would make the hardest shots with complete ease. I even wanted his competitive drive to win against the most challenging opponent.

At a young age, I embodied the wildly successful Gatorade™ commercial slogan, "I Wanna Be Like Mike." I grew up learning from my Dad that I could believe God for anything. So of course, limited by the maturity of my years. I believed God to be the same height as Michael Jordan.

But since God's Word is always right, "Who is able to do exceedingly abundantly above all that we ask or think," (Ephesians 3:20). I believed for 6'6, and God blessed me

---

[1] Proverbs 16:9

Step Out!

with 6'7. I am a full inch taller than I had petitioned Him to be. You know what that meant, right?

Confirmation!

God was on board, and I was one step closer to my dream of becoming a basketball star. I was on my way to the big time. NBA® here I come.

I focused every minute on basketball. Every extra minute I had was spent pursuing my dream of becoming a premier basketball player. As I look back, every prayer seemed to revolve around my desire to become an elite athlete. Plus, my hard work was paying off. I became the only basketball player in my high school's history to receive All-State First Team Honors.

I thought the reason for my success at the time was my desire to be the next Michael Jordan.

Around that time, there was another elite pro basketball player on the court, who was breaking records and putting up points. His name was Kobe Bryant.

During my teen years, Mr. Bryant served as just another 'confirmation' to me that God was setting me up to play professional basketball.

He too, professed to have modeled Michael Jordan's game as his motivation for getting to the NBA®. His height? 6'6.

Chapter One: Stuck

He was so good by the time he left high school, that he would forgo college and go straight to the NBA® draft that year. Can you imagine the excitement that built up inside me? I mean if he could do that in his own ability, I just knew for certain that God was going to do something even more significant for me, since I had His ability.

After all, my parents are pillars of faith. They told me the story of how I had become sick several months after my birth. And that, thankfully, following the leading of the Holy Spirit, they complied when the man of God, Kenneth Copeland, in town briefly, called for my parents to bring me to the local revival where I would be prayed for by him. By the time sickness came on my body, I was already healed.

Talk about special. I know how Joseph felt. To have his father take such care of him, reminding him that his life was a blessing from God. I was given the height I wanted. I was athletic and strong. I had the charisma and competitive nature already in my bones. In my mind, I was a perfect candidate to represent 'the faith' in the NBA®. I knew it, and God knew it too—or so I thought.

In my mind, I had already signed endorsement deals. My basketball sneaker was already on the shelves. All I had left was to decide who I was going to give the 'honor' of signing the licensing deal.

Step Out!

As the likely pick for the NBA® draft, All-Star teams, and MVP awards, it made sense for me to have an architect draft the plan for my new home. My attorney, agent, accountant, and personal physicians had already been selected. At a moment's notice, I was ready to pull them from their menial jobs to work for me. Aahhh...just thinking about the perfection of it all.

Then, poof! Out of nowhere, the endorsement deals, sneakers, MVP trophies, NBA® All-Star® games, private jets, and everything else that comes with the superstar lifestyle went up in smoke with a scalpel and an anesthesia drip.

Why am I telling you all of this?

I want you to realize that we <u>all</u> have opportunities to become stuck in a warp of failure, disappointment, loss, and fear.

In spite of this, we must keep moving forward, even when we don't know what's around the bend in the journey ahead. Sometimes all we can know is that the same God that was there through the last curve will be there with us during the next turn as well.

I think about the woman with the issue of blood.[2] She didn't allow this illness to keep her stuck. She wouldn't give up,

_____

[2] Luke 8:43-48

Chapter One: Stuck

rather she kept pushing forward. Her body had continuous blood flowing, yet, she kept going to physicians. She was determined not to stay in the same condition. She refused to remain hidden and out of sight as was the custom of that day.

Was she experiencing a challenge in her body? Yes. But she refused to just sit there in the problem. She put pressure on her body to perform the way God intended.

Currently, as I write this book, I have physical therapy appointments regularly. I don't like to go, but I do it because I refuse to get stuck.

This woman didn't start off looking for Jesus. Her focus was on natural means of healing. She was so convinced that the physicians were going to find a way to cure her until she looked around and was broke!

There are times that we sit and wallow in the reality of my situation. I have been in pain for over a month, due to the accident.

I can't tell you that it has been easy, or that I have always been positive. Having even said to myself, "How did I get to this place?"

But like the woman with the issue of blood, I push my body to do what God intended for it to do. I have started taking meetings even though the pain is still quite severe. Why?

Step Out!

I refuse to live stuck in the aftermath of the attempt on my life. It happened, I get it. But this is what I understand and believe about myself and the woman with the issue of blood. When we stay stuck in a situation after a trauma or loss, we allow the enemy to steal from us continuously. He will steal your life slowly, minute by minute many times without being recognized.

The impact on my body was designed to knock the life out of me. Literally. But instead of killing me, it altered my existence forcing me to adapt my lifestyle around the pain of the blow.

Now everything I do and every decision I have made for the last month had the pain in the center of it.

I recently preached my first message since the accident. I'm also making an effort to get back into my usual routine. This is one of the most challenging aspects of recovery— getting back to normal.

My routine has been interrupted.

I was in so much pain during my son Andrew's first birthday party. I was heartbroken that I couldn't get out of the bed. All I could do was cry. This is the son that I believed for and named after my father. He is the one that I was told was going to have down syndrome. But he came out of the womb, perfectly healthy.

Chapter One: Stuck

My daughters love for me to pick them up. They are accustomed to it, and it gives me life to hold them. The physical limitation of not being able to do that breaks my heart. And, my duties to my wife are limited.

Listen to me when I tell you that there is no part of this experience that has not affected me. And just to think that a few months ago, I was running around playing basketball with my brother.

I don't tell you this for sympathy. I'm telling you this because you need to know that no matter how bad it is for you right now, if you are a child of God, know that you don't have to stay stuck in that same place.

Open your mouth and say, **"I refuse to be stuck!"** Keep saying that over and over until you believe it.

If your business is stuck, hear yourself saying, "I refuse to be stuck in my business." No matter if it's your marriage or your business, or anything it may be, I come in faith with you that you don't have to be stuck. My faith in God is too strong to get comfortable in the middle of the worst moment of my life.

Why do I mention this to you? We must get to the root of the problem here. Maybe you thought that you were on course in one direction, but the air traffic controller is telling you that the flight plan has changed. Maybe you took a blow or received some bad news.

You might have felt rattled by the situation, but you can't camp out in the after effects of that event.

God can, and has, encouraged us that we can make it through anything because He is with us. However, the decision to live stuck or move from where we are is 100% ours to decide.

"Now a certain man was there who had an infirmity thirty-eight years. When Jesus saw him lying there and knew that he already had been *in that condition* a long time, He said to him, 'Do you want to be made well?'

The sick man answered Him, 'Sir, I have no man to put me into the pool when the water is stirred up; but while I am coming, another steps down before me.'

Jesus said to him, 'Rise, take up your bed and walk.'

And immediately the man was made well, took up his bed, and walked." (John 5:5-9 NKJV)

Jesus starts off asking this man does he even **want** to be made well. That puzzled me for a while until I realized that He must have been thinking, "If you had scooted a little each day, you would have made it to the pool by now. It's been thirty-eight years, man!"

Chapter One: Stuck

This verse doesn't indicate that this situation was the same as the man who was blind from birth[3], so that the works of God could be revealed in him.

The man by the pool could have been healed a long time ago. Then his words hit me!

He was stuck in his mind, which is why he stayed trapped in his body!

"Sir, I have no man to put me into the pool when the water is stirred up: but while I am coming, another steps down before me."

His words were the flashlight to his soul—the place where our mind, will, and emotions live. He had excuses for his limitations. Instead of pressing through the crowd, (because you can believe there was a crowd every year), he would have kept moving his body towards the water when everyone else was walking back to shore.

Faith keeps moving forward.

The same principle rings true for the woman with the issue of blood. She refused to become stuck in her mind, no matter the cost. Her payment to those physicians wasn't only about the healing of her body; it was keeping her mind free. As a result, she refused to accept that she was going

---

[3] John 9:3

to be sick for the rest of her life. And because she refused to allow her mind to get stuck, so she prohibited her body from doing the same.

I started taking meetings not because the symptoms were gone. I took meetings *because the symptoms remained.* I kept running my business from my bed because I refused to adopt a mindset that was stuck in limitations when I serve a God of the impossible. And neither should you.

"He is able to do exceedingly, abundantly, above all..." (Ephesians 3:20)

Jesus is above limitations. So that means that you and I are above constraints.

You should take a class when others say that you are too old to learn something new. You should stand when the doctors say you will never walk again. You should decide on a business name when your bank account doesn't have anything in it. You should purchase baby clothes when the tests say you can't conceive.

Force your mind to remain free from limitations, by taking actions that put pressure on your situation to bow to the limitless freedom that is available in Christ. You do this by, "Filling your thoughts on things true, noble, reputable, authentic, compelling, gracious—the best, not the worst; the beautiful, not the ugly." (Philippians 4:8 MSG)

Chapter One: Stuck

Refuse to stay in this holding pattern any longer. "You are destined for greater works than these..."[4] You house the very embodiment of God, and when you speak, everything in heaven and hell pays attention.

It's not the situations of life that cause you to become stuck. Immobility comes when you forget that,"No weapon formed against you shall prosper, (Isaiah 54:17). When you meditate on that there is nothing on earth that can stop you from breaking free from whatever has been holding you back.

---

[4] John 14:12

Step Out!

CHAPTER TWO: IT'S TIME TO SHIFT

Whenever I have gotten stuck in life, the first thing I had to do to free myself from a debilitating mindset was to change my focus.

In other words, I had to *shift* my mindset. Much like one must do when they drive a manual vehicle.

Those of us who are from the Midwest region understand what it means to get stuck in the snow. It's the last thing anyone wants to deal with when it's cold outside.

Once you get stuck, it's customary to back up a little bit, in order to go forward all the way. The same is true in life.

The Spirit of God tells us through the apostle Paul, "forgetting those things which are behind. I press [give power] towards the high calling which is in Christ Jesus, our Lord. (Philippians 3:13 *emphasis mine*)

Forgetting is a process of faith. You can learn something from the past. There is precious history there to be retained and principles to be applied to your life if you approach the past with the proper perspective.

I believe the past should help us track God's faithfulness. I regard this as a vital aspect of breaking free from periods of immobility and lack of progress. I think the past can serve as a memoir of God's dynamic power to those who reach out for assurance and faith in Him during even the most challenging times.

CAUTION: You aren't looking back so that you can figure out how to camp out there. No way. The past has a purpose of projectile if you are savvy enough to shift gears in a deliberate and focused manner.

<u>Under the Hood</u>

Once the direction of a person's mindset shifts, even the vibration of their voice lends itself to a posture of expectation. I had the belief that although my shoulder had been torn in what could only be described at the time as a rare basketball injury, my feeling that something greater was ahead of me caused a subsequent shift in the way I approached everything around me. I was determined to heal, get my shoulder healthy, and play basketball just as I had planned all along. That was until the unthinkable happened. I reinjured the same shoulder again.

I was disappointed, but God had already begun to shift my desire on the inside in a way that I didn't truly understand at the time.

Although the future wasn't entirely revealed to me, I knew that I couldn't stay stuck in a place of mental disappointment any longer.

Chapter Two: It's Time to Shift

Ultimately, I backed up enough to be thankful for all the wonderful people that I had met up to that point. For the experiences that I'd had and for my parents and family, who no matter what my occupation, would be there to love me regardless. Because to them, I was always going to be 'Jonathan' basketball superstar or not.

I grabbed that and then shifted my focus forward. It was time to push the gas on something new—I needed to focus on my education.

For those of you who are shifting, listen to me. Everyone's life is different. Do not allow yourself to get caught in a cycle of comparing your life to someone else's. God does things unique to each of us.

Even the cover of the book that you hold in your hand reflects the beautiful tapestry of variation that God uses to create something spectacular. Every gift, talent, and ability are part of a beautiful collage that He is painting with the stroke of His brush. Just sit back and enjoy the ride of His whimsical hand. We all have a depth to contribute the canvas. No one is left out of his design.

There will be times when others will tell you that you are not this or you can't do that. Stay focused on Jesus. He is the author and finisher of your faith.[5] He started the journey

---

[5] Hebrews 12:2

with you, and He will finish it with you. Keep getting your direction from the Holy Spirit. Stop doubting yourself.

There are going to be times when a voice inside of you will echo thoughts of doubt and inadequacy. It will raise the volume to get your attention. **Ignore it.** I'm telling you, just ignore those voices that seek to strip not only your confidence in God but your confidence in yourself.

I can't tell you how many times I felt like a failure for not achieving the basketball success I had dreamed of and worked toward for so long. However, what I found was that even when those voices were the loudest; I could still hear that 'still small voice' telling me with assurance that I am good enough and that I am capable. There is no doubt in my mind that if you listen, you will hear those same words being spoken to you.

Press Forward

Look, the unknown might not be known to us, but we can rest in the fact that God is fully aware of every day that is recorded in our lives. He has already gone before us. He knows the length of your days![6] What we don't know about tomorrow, He already does.

---

[6] Proverbs 3:2

Chapter Two: It's Time to Shift

"I press towards the mark [goal] for the prize of the high calling of God in Christ Jesus." (Philippians 3:14)

God has plans for your life that have been crafted for you. Although our lives might intersect during different spaces in time, our goal should always be to focus on and propel ourselves in the direction of what God has designated for us to accomplish for him.

Paul was explicitly saying that his actions were directly focused on the calling or purpose before him. He never mentions anyone else in these verses. The central characters are the Father, Jesus, and himself. Making us aware of who we are and whose we are. A critical component to sustaining us, especially during a season of shifting.

A New Gear

Ok, so you've had a lapse of focus that subsequently had you stuck in life for a while. Look it happens. Don't make the mistake of getting stuck again, whining about 'how long' it took you to shift your gears. Come on you're better than that.

The season ahead must be focused on getting results. You have some ground to make up. But that doesn't mean that it can't be done. God has a way of restoring time right before your eyes. Where it took you forever to get one thing accomplished, you can look up, and it has only taken a few days or a couple of weeks.

Shift into a cruising altitude. Focused solely on God and His purposes and promises for you. Keeping your heart and posture fixed in expectation to see the manifestation of the things that He has wanted to do in your life all along.

There will be challenges ahead. But hopefully one of the things that you grabbed in the survey of your past experiences was the assurance that you are resilient. He built you that way. There is nothing that you will go through that He is not able and willing to bring you through.

You are still alive to tell the story, so you must know that there is something incredibly powerful that God wants to get from your life. Knowing that, is what encouraged me through painkillers and sleepless nights.

Remember, you were created by Him, through Him, and for Him. He has taken great care to develop your life into a masterpiece that He can be proud to display. You might not see it right now. But as I look back, He has taken my most challenging life situations and created an incredible work of art out of them. So you can be confident that He is doing the same thing for you. You only need to trust His plan for your life.

Chapter Two: It's Time to Shift

"For we are His workmanship [His own master work, a work of art], created in Christ Jesus [reborn from above—spiritually transformed, renewed, ready to be used] for good works, which God prepared [for us] beforehand [taking paths which He set], so that we would walk in them [living the good life which He prearranged and made ready for us]." (Ephesians 2:10 AMP)

Step Out!

CHAPTER THREE: FEAR FACTOR

Have you ever heard the saying, "Face your fears?" Well, in this case, I'm telling you to kick your fears in the teeth.

I've always heard people say that fear is the opposite of faith. But it's more than that. Fear is a foul spirit dispatched by satan to paralyze you so that you can't move forward with God's plan for your life with liberty.

"For God did not give us a spirit of timidity *or* cowardice *or* fear, but [He has given us a spirit] of power and of love and of sound judgment *and* personal discipline [abilities that result in a calm, well-balanced mind and self-control]." (2 Timothy 1:7 AMP)

Fear is based in selfishness and self-centeredness, because it places the attention on how weak you are instead of how incredibly capable God is. And when you do that, there is no way you are going to slay a giant or kill a bear.[7]

The spirit of fear can only be annihilated by how you wield your sword [the Word of God]. Meaning the effectiveness of how well you operate in and with what you know. It's that simple.

---

[7] 1 Samuel 17:34-36

Step Out!

Goliath was toast because David knew that God was strong enough to take him down. [8]

My accident in Costa Rica was supposed to make me afraid to do anything else—drive, travel, work, or move about at all. But I will continue to do all those things because of what I know.

I know that God is able to keep me from falling and to present me faultless before the Almighty.[9]

I know that greater is He that is in me than he that is in the world. [10]

I know the One who holds the world together by the word of His power. [11]

I know who lives on the inside of me.

Nothing that satan has whispered in your ear is based in reality. The 'I can't' chants are all lies based on fear. It's all lies—every little bit of it.

The Word of God says, "You can," in every line. But it took my Dad to have a heart attack for the paralyzing effects of fear to be made real to me.

---

[8] 1 Samuel 17
[9] Jude 1:24
[10] I John 4:4
[11] Hebrews 1:3

Chapter Three: Fear Factor

In the summer of 2005, my father experienced a heart attack. The first thing I remember from that day was my mother performing our annual Catechism graduation mostly on her own that Sunday morning. After service, I distinctly remember standing outside my Dad's office door thinking, "Something isn't right. Something is wrong."

I watched as the physicians and nurses that attend to our church, cared for him. Finally, my mother said, "We are going to the hospital."

Even in that action, I should have realized that my father would be fine. Because while in a moment of crisis, he was still standing on the Word of God. He refused to allow anyone to call an ambulance to pick him up from the church. He demanded to be driven in a car instead.

His stand was simple, "It will never be said that the man of faith was driven away with sirens flashing at 10100 Grand River."

Concerned not about his reputation, but rather, that God's integrity was at stake. Not at any moment giving yield to his body. He 'allowed' himself to be driven to the hospital, not picked up in a truck.

I do remember him looking into my eyes, obviously seeing the fright on my face.

He said, "I'm going to be fine. Everything is okay." I thought to myself, "You don't look fine. You don't look okay."

There is a frozen chill that fear brings that will incapacitate logic and your emotional center. Fear takes no prisoners. It was a chilling experience to think that I wouldn't see my Dad again.

In the same way I was thinking that day, so are many of you. You are thinking worst case. But if we focus on the attack, instead of looking at God, we essentially surrender to the fear of a negative end in any situation.

My Dad is a man of faith; through and through. If he said that he was okay, then his track record with God should have been enough for me to grab hold to. But at twenty-two years old, I couldn't process anything beyond, my own personal Superman being hit with some kryptonite, and I wasn't sure if he would come back from it.

The force of fear drove me home that day. While my family was locked in faith at the hospital surrounding my Dad with love, I was at home watching the movie, "Kill Bill" (of all things).

This is what I did while I tried to process the magnitude of life without my father there beside me. Can you see how irrational fear can be?

Chapter Three: Fear Factor

The illogical reactions of fear will have you looking and acting contrary to what's in your heart. My siblings were calling, asking, "Where are you?"

I was so scared until I had zoned out. As they were asking me my location, I couldn't fully answer intelligently. I was a mess!

Full of tears, sorrow, and grief. In my mind, there was no way he was making it out of that hospital alive. Then I moved into pity. I just knew that there were so many more experiences to be had and lessons to be learned.

I can't even tell you the roller coaster I was on that day. The effects of fear will stop you in your tracks. As I said before, "Fear is birthed in selfishness." It thrives in self-centeredness. Here I was focused on me, while my dad was in the hospital. He was the one having chest pains. And yet somehow, I had twisted the situation and made it about me. How pathetic is that?

When you want to do a fear check of yourself, start right there. When you make every situation and decision about you, or you find yourself unable to move forward because of how *you* feel. Or because of how *you* will be perceived or you, you, you. If every sentence starts, I, I, I, then I can almost guarantee **you** that **you** are walking in fear.

Step Out!

Finally, after an extended amount of time, I started asking myself, "What if this is it? What if these are my dad's last moments? What am I doing here and not there with him?"

Later that evening I went to the hospital to see him. It was determined by that time that he'd had a heart attack and was resting. For most people that would have been the end of the story. But my Dad **is** Superman. Not just to me, but to many.

He was driven to the hospital on a Sunday evening, by Thursday afternoon, he was running One-In-Worship, a multi-denominational worship conference held at Ford Field—testifying in front of thousands of people about the faithfulness of God.

My Dad demonstrated how to step out that day and became a catalyst that pushed me to step out too!

I am convinced, that if we want to see the hand of God move in our lives; if we're going to witness things restored; miracles take place; and people's lives changed; it is because we too step out of fear into the faith that only God provides.

"But without faith [confidence in God] it is impossible to please him." (Hebrews 11:6 NIV)

The remarkable reaction to what happened before my eyes was that my Dad took a blow that day. However, he kept on moving. It was a moment of shifting for me. I realized that fear could no longer be a factor.

I, myself, stepped out myself after witnessing his bold stance of faith. I realized at that moment that a retired basketball player was never my motivation. Not really. My motivation was to make my Dad proud. I thought being the best basketball player in the world was what I needed to do to fulfill that desire.

At three years old, I was watching my Dad's beloved Detroit Pistons team all the time. His excitement, my excitement over a win or the disappointment over a loss was bonding and binding for us. I was three, and I always wanted to have that connection with my father. His bold stand of faith made me want to be like him even more. It was never really about Mike. It was always about Andrew.

Shortly after graduation, I started working at the church where my parents pastor full-time. My moment had come to eliminate fear and step out on faith.

It's NOT About You

What is it that God is beaconing you to step out to do? What area are you selfish about with your time, talents, and abilities? What perceived weaknesses does God want to use for His purpose that you are saying "no" to on a regular basis?

Step Out!

My father's actions during that process said one thing very clear, "It's not about me." Everyone would have understood if he wanted to forgo One-In-Worship that year. Attendees and guests would have prayed and been amenable to his not attending or sitting through the conference to rest and recover.

Instead, he demonstrated that it is about others seeing that when God is with you—you've got to step out—be on the stage. Stand out in faith and trust God. He knows that the only way that other people will see that God can be trusted and counted faithful to His Word is to see someone in the earth do that very thing.

As I said, his example did that for me.

As I sat in the home theater, I was completely gripped with fear. Fast forward a few months later, and I followed my pastor's example and stepped out on faith too!

How did that happen?

By watching someone else keep on going, stepping out, and moving forward with God's plan for his life.

Guess what? That's why fear can't be a factor. It just can't be. There are people waiting for you to grab yourself. Take the hit but keep on going. It's the only way that others around you will be able to do the same.

Chapter Three: Fear Factor

That's the real agenda here. When fear is a factor, it stops you from stepping out on faith in your own life. It also freezes the progression of others who need to see faith in action up close and personal.

Remind yourself that there is nothing that could ever stop God's plan from coming to pass in your life.

Let's stay determined to forget fear because it [fear] is not a factor. Not a factor at all.

Like my Dad always says, **"Death to your fears and life to your faith."**

Step Out!

CHAPTER FOUR: OPEN YOUR MOUTH

As I lay in my bed recuperating from the accident in Costa Rica, initially I didn't say a lot of anything that would begin to push my body towards healing.

However, I smelled like smoke and looked like ash. Everything I said was contrary to where I wanted to be. I kept rehearsing where I was. Looking in the mirror, I didn't speak those things that be not as though they were.[12]

My spirit felt as if it had been jolted just as hard as my body. I felt like everything was disjointed, my tongue included.

Of course, I was listening to the Word of God. I was tuning into the *Finding Your Focus* television network (fyf.tv) regularly to keep the Word of God in my ears.

The Word tells us that faith comes by hearing, so I knew that I was going to have to listen to the Word of God to build my confidence to the point of confessing it for results.

I mean, I knew that, but when I look back, I realized that I was hearing, but I wasn't listening.

Certainly I don't profess to know everything, but I do know there is a significant difference between hearing and listening.

---

[12] Romans 4:17

Step Out!

Hearing is the audible distinction of sounds. It is not the same as responding in action to what something says—listening.

I heard the Word in my sleep, but I wasn't responding to the Word in my heart. There was no way to get my mouth to take audible action to speak what I heard without fully processing it first.

My two beautiful daughters love to run through the house. I have told them over and over to stop running in the house. When I ask them, "Why are you running?" My daughter Cristina is quick to say, "I don't know."

I ask her, "What have I told you?"

"Stop running."

Fifteen minutes later, what do you think they are doing again?

Running.

Which means they heard what I said, they just weren't listening to the message.

Typically, when a person is listening, they are looking for cues to make a physical response to what they heard. Each of us must ask ourselves, especially in times of hardship and challenge, "Did I hear or am I listening to the Word of God?" When we start looking for ways to engage a physical action to what we hear in the Word. I can guarantee you that it's going to start with your mouth.

Sometimes we hear, but we don't *take the time* to listen. I believe that I would have been out of pain a lot sooner, had I really listened to what the Word of God was saying to me.

It took me listening to my daughter, Lillian, memorizing Luke 24:1 for school to bring, Luke 24:6 to life for me again!

"He is not here, but is risen! Remember **how** He spoke to you when He was still in Galilee," (Luke 24:6-7)

The 'how' jumped out at me. Most of the translations have the word 'how' He said it to them. Not 'what' He said. How did He say it to them? I believe He told them in faith!

The verse was reminding me that the manner He said it was just as important as what He said. Meaning that there is a 'how to speak faith!'

If I had been listening to the Word, I would have spoken the Word a lot louder and a lot sooner. I would have been trying to stand up and move my arm—doing things I couldn't do before.

I would have spoken to my body and taken authority over the pain, commanding my nerves to calm down and bones to be healed.

Step Out!

I had to remember not only *what* he said. I had to remember *what* He did!

That's the power of what listening will do for you. Listening will always bring you back to what Jesus did.

Jesus already took nerve pain on the cross for us. He already dealt with sore bones and bruises. He had more open wounds than I can count. He already felt the physical aftermath of being thrown to the ground violently in the dark and on a dusty road. Nothing I am going through was new to Him. He already took it all and rose beyond that point.

The revelation of that gave me freedom that day! Meaning my identification for healing is that He has taken authority over pain.

Nerve pain was tackled on the cross!

Numbness was defeated through His blood sacrifice!

That's how faith works! We must remember what He said and *how* He said it. That's what we latch our faith on. I had to remind myself what was spoken over me at my ordination, "That I would lay hands on the sick and they would recover. That I would lay hands on the dead and they would live again."

Chapter Four: Open Your Mouth

I had to remember the words that were spoken over me since birth. I had to remember *how* He said them as much as *what* He had already spoken over me.

I have faith in what God has already said concerning me!

Faith demands a corresponding action to document its power. Our tongue should be a reactive tool of the Spirit. When we speak, God is speaking. We have the power of death and life in our mouths.[13]

That's what happens when you listen. Listening to the Word begins to shift your mindset, and consequently, your mouth gets involved.

Instead of focusing in on the Word I was hearing and listening for the cues of my healing, I was complaining, looking like fire and smelling like smoke. I sounded defeated—yet I have been called with an anointing to preach and declare that yokes be broken, burdens removed, and sickness flee.

Do you see how far the effects of the enemy's attacks can reach if we aren't vigilant to get back on the Word of God quickly?

Let's get real for a second. We have all had times where we know what we should do but don't. I knew that I should

---

[13] Proverbs 18:21

be speaking the Word, but I wasn't. Thankfully, I have a family that is rooted and grounded in the Word of God, and they are speaking faith and praying faith and living by faith every single day.

But even with my wife's love and care, my Mom sending me verses of scripture, my Dad preaching and teaching, and my brother and sisters support and encouragement, I was still sitting there in what was the equivalent of sackcloth and ashes.

A lot of you don't have what I have in a support system. I regret that and understand that you may have a different set of supporting cast around you. But you can't stay in bed, any longer. Sometimes, all you have is to speak the Word with tears running down your face. I'm being transparent here. I had to.

Even with the beautiful family I have, when I couldn't stop the pain long enough to drift off to sleep. I had to open my mouth and confess the Word of God.

It is essential that you are selective about who and what you listen to and never allow negativity to get the last word. Never let the conversation with yourself end in defeat. You are more than victorious through Jesus.

I've had the same fight. Don't minimize what I am telling you here. I am sharing my story with you, to let you know that just because I stand on a pulpit doesn't mean that I get a pass on doing what the Word says. That includes guarding my tongue against the negative thoughts that try to invade my vocal cords. It gets real sometimes.

But, here's what we need to be doing—opening our mouths to tell everyone we can, about the wonderful things God has done for us *in spite of* the situations that have occurred in our lives.

We need to open our mouths and declare the faithfulness of God, *regardless* of the challenges we face. We should be rehearsing thoughts of gratitude for His hand on our shoulders, keeping us steady during the process.

You see He is still saying, "Step out," even when we are determined to shut in.

God is saying to you and to me collectively, "C'mon now! Get up! Get going! I have things for you to do. It's time to ease back into your normal routine. Declare your healing— open your mouth and take the medicine of My Word. I've given you the promise that if you declare it, all of heaven will back you. Let's go!"

My father recently said something in one of his sermons that stuck with me, "You can't, but He can!"

Step Out!

God is not even asking you to do the work of stepping out. He has already done the job for you. His requirement is that you believe Him throughout the process.

I know it's not always going to look easy and there will be moments when all you can do is throw it all on God!

Yet, even with what lies ahead, we must determine that we're going to stay in faith. We're never going to stop declaring the faithfulness of our God, no matter the sadness or disappointment.

CHAPTER FIVE: GET UP

My dad asked me what I considered a ridiculous question at the time. "Do you want to preach?"

I was thinking, "Are you serious? Do you see what I'm going through? I'm in pain. I can barely walk. Do I want to preach? Not a chance."

I didn't say any of those things to him that day. Instead, I respectfully declined, limped back home, took some pain meds, and went to sleep.

Of course, my dad knew the severity of my pain. I'm sure he could see it written all over my face. Just like I looked in his office and could tell something was wrong that day when I was twenty-two years old, during my father's heart attack. He could tell that I wasn't 'faking' the pain.

What I soon realized was that I mistook the familiar audible sound of my father's voice and missed the voice of God. "Do you want to preach?" wasn't a request from my earthly father, it was an invitation of faith from my heavenly Father.

I heard the question he asked me that day. What I didn't listen for was _who_ was asking the question.

Don't miss a Word from God because you are stubbornly focused on staying in the place that you are in. There is not some righteous reward for murmuring and complaining through your situation.

My earthly father and my heavenly Father were both trying to get me to step out of where I was at the time.

You see when I did preach a few weeks later, I stood through an entire sermon, laid hands on the sick, and was still standing throughout the end of service. I even fellowshipped with the congregation before I went home that day.

The Father was inviting me to take my eyes off the circumstance and place my eyes back on His plan for my life. Then and only then, would I be able to see the full manifestation of my healing with the same swiftness that my Dad did.

What did my dad do? He immediately put the Word to work in his life by taking actions that agreed with his faith in God.

"Worship the Lord your God, and his blessing will be on your food and water, I will take away sickness from among you." (Exodus 23:25 NIV)

Can you track the pattern here?

Confidence in the Word is vital when you are going through challenging situations in life. I should have placed more

Chapter Five: Get Up

faith in the Word than what I saw in the mirror. Yes, my hand and arm were swollen and numb. Yes, sometimes my leg didn't have feeling in it. But instead of declaring the Word over my body, like I watched my dad do after having a heart attack, I murmured, complained, and slept.

I couldn't get my mouth involved because my heart was not there yet.

The moment I listened, really listened, I agreed to preach at our West (second) church location. I walked so slowly to the stand. I gingerly stood up and began to minister the Word, and that's when I felt some strength come.

After that service, I told the deacon that was driving me around that I wanted to go home and sleep. But I knew that saying "yes" to God meant seeing the entire day through. So off to main church campus we went!

I arrived in the sanctuary and sat in the back around 9:45am that morning. As one of the ministers led a prayer for the morning service, it was then I knew that I would be preaching this service too!

When my dad came downstairs and walked by me, he whispered, "Don't worry about the offering message—I've got it.

My response, "Good, because I'm going to preach the service."

Step Out!

Half-way through service, I felt stronger than I had since the accident took place. Ladies and gentlemen that is what happens when you step out. I didn't want to preach. I didn't even have a sermon prepared. But it was time to come off the bench and take my life off pause.

Since that Sunday morning, I have felt more and more healing manifest in my body. I tell you that there is never going to be a time when you regret taking a step of faith in God's direction—never. I mean there is nothing like stepping out on the author and finisher of our faith.

You are not alone. Don't forget that. We are all required to take a step of faith if we want to see the healing, deliverance or miracles manifest in our lives today.

CHAPTER SIX: SOLID FOUNDATION

"'Lord, if it's you,' Peter replied, 'tell me to come to you on the water.'

'Come,' he said.

Then Peter got down out of the boat, walked on the water and came toward Jesus." (Matthew 14:28-29 NIV)

If there is anyone who makes me step out on God's Word— it's my father.

He has been demonstrating what it means to be a *Wet Water Walker* all my life. All I know is that if Jesus says, "Andrew, come." He is leaping out of the boat to get to Jesus. I genuinely don't know anything else.

I'm so glad that I have a man in my life who I can continuously see God's hand in his. I get to see God in him. I have a front row seat of God manifesting Himself to my father on a regular basis.

i have been able to see him speak to the same body that had a heart condition with no reoccurrence since. You see my father is always, always, always trying to be like Jesus. He is not focused on celebrity or notoriety. He is focused on Jesus.

I can't tell you that weapons (including trials and tribulations) will not be formed. Or that things won't happen to knock you off balance. But what I can assure you is that they won't prosper against you—because there is no way for them to flourish in your life.

A weapon can't prosper against a God that tells you in advance that He sees the person making the weapon. How awesome is that? I learned these foundational principles from my parents and others in the ministry that I respect who have impacted my life significantly.

They have reaffirmed the Word, as I matured into the understanding that we must walk in faith, stand in faith, speak in faith, and truly step out on faith, there is no way that we are going to see signs, wonders, and miracles happen in our world.

It's not enough for me to know that we are all required to begin to operate from the revelation that there is nothing that can stop God's plan from coming to pass.

Now that I've had various experiences to look back on, I can say, "I'm still here. Nothing that happened stopped me from moving forward."

I have a wife. I have three kids. I'm a pastor. God's will for my life has continued to unfold and develop. I'm sure you can look back and see His will unfolding in your life, if not, step closer.

We are ripe for God to use us in incredible ways. He is waiting for us to lift our leg muscles and take the first step

Chapter Six: Solid Foundation

towards Him, so He can expose us to the greatness of His desire.

I am so excited because I know that you are as ready as I am to see the manifested presence of God in your life. There is no firmer foundation to step on than the One who has risen from death and can consume the fire of adversity that you feel like is surrounding you.

All the flames, smoke and soot can't stop you! I felt like I had flames burning up to my ears. I just knew it was over for me. I couldn't see beyond the blaze that had engulfed me at times. I was toast. The situation was too big for me to handle. And then I remembered that God is a consuming fire!

He did it for three Hebrew boys,[14] which means He has obligated Himself to do the same for us. We have a better covenant—a blood covenant. If you have given your heart to Jesus, you have been purchased with the precious blood of God's gift of love to the world. You can stand on His willingness to absorb all the energy and power of the fire that is threatening to destroy you.

Jesus was obedient all the way through death, so He has us covered every way we turn. He has already been there and done that. He's fighting for us. He has already equipped

---

[14] Daniel 3:16-18

Step Out!

us for victory. He is our solid rock. We can stand forever because when we step out, we're standing in Him. [15]

---

[15] Acts 17:28

CHAPTER SEVEN: EVERY LITTLE STEP

Remember the shift we talked about earlier?

It's real, and everyone who is on the path to greatness will make it multiple times throughout their lifetime.

We aren't called to be average. We are called to be great and to fulfill His plans for our life. We are all called to be great!

But why? Why are we called to be great? Is it to satisfy some alter ego madness that we have about ourselves? No! We are called to greatness because He is great! Everything the Father does is excellent, and if we are to imitate Him, then we are to reflect a life that demonstrates, not the capabilities of who we are, but instead of who He is.

Called to Greatness

"For we are His workmanship [His own master work, a work of art], created in Christ Jesus [reborn from above— spiritually transformed, renewed, ready to be used] for good works, which God prepared [for us] beforehand [taking paths which He set], so that we would walk in them [living the good life which He prearranged and made ready for us]." (Ephesians 2:10 AMP)

My first day back in the pulpit, there was a fifteen-minute span of time where all I kept hearing was, "You'd better take your seat now."

Step Out!

I read the above verse before I came to church that day and it reminded me that I don't belong to myself and neither do you. We belong to Jesus—it is His hand upon us.

Some of you don't think that you have a gift. You don't believe that God has designed something special. Listen, that's defeated thinking.

Know right now that God has *good works* for you to do. Isn't that exciting? He predestined and planned beforehand your success in life. God has a master plan. Wait for the Spirit of God to give you direction. Don't try to run ahead of Him, know that He has already ordered your steps.

I had to ask myself, "How in the world am I sitting here day after day, asking God, 'Why has this happened to me?'" There are no good works coming from laying in the bed all day asking God, "Why?"

I know I'm not alone in this regard, am I? Don't shy away now—you know that you've asked why too!

But, let me ask you the question that I had to ask myself? "What has asking, 'why' ever gotten you?"

Hold on, let me answer that one, "Nothing!"

Asking God, "why" to which I still haven't received a response, was a waste of valuable time. Because all it does is stop us from moving forward and stepping out. It doesn't really matter why at this point, does it?

Ultimately, the 'why' will stop you from listening in anticipation for the Holy Spirit to speak and that's not what we want, is it? No.

Whatever trauma you experienced, or loss or attack you have gone through, it happened already, and you have lived to tell the story.

My thinking shifted from "Why?" to "What?"

I should have been asking all along, "What's next?"

Asking God, "What's next?" puts you in position to be blessed. It places you in step with what God has in front of you. I know that my 'next' involves me telling the testimony of how my life was miraculously spared in another country on a dark road from the most bizarre accident I've ever heard.

That might not be your story, but you have something that God wants to say to the world through you, too.

<u>The Good Life</u>

"God created us like a work of art through Christ Jesus for good works that he prearranged beforehand that set us on paths for a good life that He made ready for us." (emphasis mine)

Step Out!

There is a good life ready for us as we step out and proceed on the journey that God has already arranged in His plans for us on earth together.

No matter what comes, we have no need to fear, because God has already prepared our victory in advance.[16]

Make a new commitment today to no longer make decisions for the heck of it. Understanding that God has a predetermined destiny for us should give us a tremendous amount of security as we walk out the days of our lives.

Impact Your World

Some steps could be long strides, while others might be tiny movements. Either way, the focus is clear, it's time to balance your belief in God's desire to use you to make an impact on the earth.

It's time to stop hiding, peeking behind the curtain, watching everyone else get in the flow of what God is doing in the world. It's your turn to arise and step out on faith ready to fulfill the kingdom mandate of reaching *your* city, *your* nation, and *your* world for Jesus Christ.

There is no reason to delay action.

"No time like the present," I always say.

---

[16] **Psalm 20:1-2**

Chapter Seven: Every Little Step

So let's take that first step together, by praying that the Father be glorified in our lives and we step out in faith on His will for our lives!

Before you pray this prayer, ask a friend or family member to join with you in taking the steps towards a new journey that starts today. I believe that we are a community. We are stronger together in every way.

Once you have at least one person (parents, it could be your child) let's lock our focus on God together as we Step Out today!

Let's turn the page together.

On the next page, you will find the prayer that we are going to recite together as we step out on faith in God and His promises to us.

THE PROGRESS PRAYER

Father, I thank You that I can come boldly before Your throne and obtain mercy in the time of need, indecision, or stagnation. I am humbled by Your love and care for me. There is no circumstance, situation, or setback that You cannot bring me back from. And no distance that You will not extend Your arm to bring me into Your purpose and plan for my life. The life that You have given to me.

I submit myself to You today; mind, body, and soul. I take by faith the help that You send from Your Holy hill. Receiving with gladness the garment of praise for the spirit of heaviness for every challenge that I face.

Today, I take my first step of faith towards Your will. Forgetting those things which are behind me, I reach for Your calling in my life. Overwhelmed with excitement and anticipation of the manifestations of Your faithfulness flourishing in my life.

I pray for those who are joining with me to see the same awakening of faith in their life. I come into agreement with them that they receive courage to move towards the promises that You've made to them without hesitation or reservation.

Receive this prayer as our first action as we step out on You! In Jesus Name, Amen.

STEP OUT! Community Sign-Up

	Relation	Name	Date
1.		_____	___/___/___
2.		_____	___/___/___
3.		_____	___/___/___
4.		_____	___/___/___
5.		_____	___/___/___
6.		_____	___/___/___
7.		_____	___/___/___
8.		_____	___/___/___
9.		_____	___/___/___
10.		_____	___/___/___
11.		_____	___/___/___
12.		_____	___/___/___
13.		_____	___/___/___
14.		_____	___/___/___
15.		_____	___/___/___

Track who else has stepped out on faith, and prayed The Progress Prayer with you!

ABOUT THE AUTHOR

At an early age, one could witness that Jonathan Andrew Merritt had the presence of God's spirit moving in his life. Prophecy was spoken over Jonathan even before his birth. His father, Bishop Andrew Merritt, prophesied that this son, Jonathan, would be born on his birthday of November 28, and it was so. Jonathan, like his father, shares the same birth date of the 28th of November.

The Spirit of God was, once again, moving on Jonathan's behalf, when on the sixth day of his birth, he was anointed with oil and dedicated by Brother Kenneth Copeland before thirteen thousand believers. Brother Copeland prayed that Jonathan would walk in faith, walk in love, walk in the Word of God; and he declared that he would not know the sting and hurt of sickness nor disease. A few months later, Jonathan's physician gave a report that he would have to take medication throughout his life. This was not the report of God and Jonathan was healed.

Jonathan is anointed with several ministry gifts, including administration, leadership, teacher, and pastor. He confesses that he knows he is blessed because he was raised in a loving and Godly home and the Spirit of God was always present.

Although he is at the young age of 35, he has experienced a lifetime of learning to love the Lord, trust in the Lord, put the Lord first in all things, follow the leading of the Holy Spirit, and walk by faith. He has watched his parents touch the hearts, minds, and souls of their 6,000-member congregation. As the son of Bishop Andrew and Pastor Viveca C. Merritt, the founders of Straight Gate International Church in Detroit, Jonathan has learned many valuable lessons from those whom he describes as, "the greatest role models a son could have"— his parents. They have shown him great humility, strength, and perseverance, and inspired in him a passion for Christ.

He has walked in the vision God gave his father more than almost 40 years ago, "to reach the city, nation, and world for Jesus Christ." He realizes that this vision can transform the lives of millions from darkness into the marvelous light of Jesus Christ. Jonathan knows that God has called him to be a part of fulfilling this vision and to give voice to the vision for the next generation. God is a generational God. Jonathan has devoted himself to the Ministry of Helps and has assisted in the Music and Media Ministry.

In obedience to the will of God, Jonathan Andrew Merritt was ordained as a minister in February 2010. In May of 2010, he began serving as the church administrator. Three years later in 2013, his additional assignment was Pastor of Straight Gate International Church–West, located in West Bloomfield, Michigan.

About the Author

In 2014, he assumed the responsibility of Administrator of the Joseph Business School-Straight Gate International Church campus site. He is also a board member of *Give Merit*, a non-profit organization.

Jonathan is a graduate of West Bloomfield High School and is the only basketball player in the school's history to receive All-State First Team Honors. He is a 2005 graduate of the University of Michigan with a BA degree in General Studies and a concentration in Business. He is a co-owner of a thriving coffee shop, Narrow Way Café & Shop, located in the city of Detroit. He was married on October 24, 2010, to his lovely wife Tatianna, and they are the parents of two incredible and beautiful young daughters, Lillian Grace and Cristina Faith, and a son, Andrew II.

For more information about the author please visit www.jonathanamerritt.com.

CPSIA information can be obtained
at www.ICGtesting.com
Printed in the USA
FFOW01n1229030418
46145688-47283FF